CONTENTS

❦ Lake Classic Short Stories ❧

"The universe is made of stories, not atoms."
—Muriel Rukeyser

"The story's about you."
—Horace

Everyone loves a good story. It is hard to think of a friendlier introduction to classic literature. For one thing, short stories are *short*—quick to get into and easy to finish. Of all the literary forms, the short story is the least intimidating and the most approachable.

Great literature is an important part of our human heritage. In the belief that this heritage belongs to everyone, *Lake Classic Short Stories* are adapted for today's readers. Lengthy sentences and paragraphs are shortened. Archaic words are replaced. Modern punctuation and spellings are used. Many of the longer stories are abridged. In all the stories,

5

painstaking care has been taken to preserve the author's unique voice.

Lake Classic Short Stories have something for everyone. The hundreds of stories in the collection cover a broad terrain of themes, story types, and styles. Literary merit was a deciding factor in story selection. But no story was included unless it was as enjoyable as it was instructive. And special priority was given to stories that shine light on the human condition.

Each book in the *Lake Classic Short Stories* is devoted to the work of a single author. Little-known stories of merit are included with famous old favorites. Taken as a whole, the collected authors and stories make up a rich and diverse sampler of the story-teller's art.

Lake Classic Short Stories guarantee a great reading experience. Readers who look for common interests, concerns, and experiences are sure to find them. Readers who bring their own gifts of perception and appreciation to the stories will be doubly rewarded.

❦ Charles W. Chesnutt ❧
(1858–1932)

About the Author

Charles Waddell Chesnutt grew up in the aftermath of the Civil War. Born in Cleveland, Ohio, he was raised in Fayetteville, North Carolina. He was the son of free blacks and the grandson of a wealthy white tobacco merchant.

As light-skinned people, his parents had some advantages in the color-conscious South. There was always food on the table. And there was always enough money to keep their bright and studious son in school. But even as a child, he was keenly aware of negative attitudes toward people of color. All of his life he resented this prejudice. And in all of his writings, he worked to expose its hypocrisy and cruel consequences.

A man of many talents, Chesnutt became a lawyer and founded a court-reporting business in Cleveland. His secret goal, however, was to "strike an entering wedge in the literary world." This he did in 1887 when his first short story was published in *Atlantic Monthly* magazine. He went on to write two well-reviewed collections of short stories and three novels.

Chesnutt's powerful and moving stories were a shock and a lesson to mainstream America. His artistry with the short story form did indeed "strike a wedge." By confronting racism head-on, he pioneered new ground in fiction writing. Never before had a black American writer presented such a clear picture of those who live close to the "color line."

Today, literary historians credit Chesnutt with "almost singlehandedly" establishing a truly African-American tradition in the short story. His work has inspired generations of black writers.

If you enjoy realistic stories about interesting people in difficult situations, you'll like Charles W. Chesnutt.

The Wife of His Youth

How much claim does the past have on the present? In this tender story of love and loyalty, Mr. Ryder faces a test of honor.

SHE LOOKED LIKE A BIT OF THE OLD PLANTATION LIFE.

The Wife of His Youth

Mr. Ryder was planning a grand ball. There were several reasons why this was a good time for such an event.

Mr. Ryder could be called the dean of the Blue Vein Society. The first Blue Veins were a little group of colored persons in a Northern city. Shortly after the Civil War, they had organized as a club. The purpose of the club was to set up high social standards among its members. Outsiders grumbled about it. They said that only light-skinned colored people were allowed to join. A member's skin had to be light enough to show blue veins. Darker-skinned people were resentful.

The Blue Veins *claimed*, however, to have only two rules for membership. These were character and culture. People like Mr. Ryder could easily explain why its members were light-colored. They said that light-skinned persons often had better opportunities to qualify for membership.

Some people attacked the society. They said that it was a glaring example of prejudice. And wasn't prejudice what had caused the colored race so much suffering? But these very same people changed their minds if *they* became members. Then they said that the society was a blessed guide through the social wilderness. Most of its members had been born free. But one or two of the older members had come up from slavery.

Mr. Ryder was the leader of the society. He preserved its traditions. He shaped its rules. He made sure there was always plenty of entertainment, so the members would stay interested.

There were other reasons for Mr. Ryder's popularity. While he was not as white as some of the Blue Veins, his looks were distinguished. His features were fine, and his hair was nearly straight. He was always neatly dressed. He had perfect manners and the highest of morals.

Mr. Ryder had come to Groveland as a young man. At first he had gone to work as a messenger for a railroad company. Over the years he worked up to the job of clerk. Nature had given him a fine mind, and he read a great deal. Poetry was his passion. He could recite whole pages of the great English poets.

Mr. Ryder owned a very comfortable house on a respectable street. His house was handsomely furnished. It contained a good library, a piano, and some fine artwork. Usually a young couple lived with him. They kept him company, as Mr. Ryder was a single man. At one time Mr. Ryder had been regarded as quite a catch. Many young ladies and their mothers had tried hard to capture him.

But not until Mrs. Molly Dixon visited
Groveland had he ever considered
marrying.

Mrs. Dixon had come to Groveland
in the spring. Before the summer was
over, the pretty widow had won Mr.
Ryder's heart. She was a pleasant,
attractive woman, much younger than
he. She was whiter than he, and better
educated. In Washington, she belonged
to the best colored society in the country.
Her husband had been a government
clerk there, and she had taught school.
Her husband had left her a large sum
of money.

Of course she had been eagerly
welcomed to the Blue Vein Society. She
took part in all its activities. She had
come to Groveland to visit friends. But
then she had found both the town and
the people to her liking. So she had
stayed on.

Right from the beginning she had
encouraged Mr. Ryder's attentions. A
younger and less cautious man would

have already spoken to her. But he had made up his mind. He had only to choose the moment when he would ask her to become his wife. So he had decided to give a ball in her honor. At some time during the evening, he would offer her his heart and hand.

Mr. Ryder wanted his ball to be perfect. It had to outshine any party that had ever taken place in Groveland. It had to be worthy of the lady of honor. And its guests must set an example for the future. Lately he had noticed that the Society's standards were slipping.

"I have no race prejudice," Mr. Ryder would say. "But we people of mixed blood have a responsibility. We are caught between the upper and the lower classes. One class doesn't want us yet—but it might accept us in time. The other class would welcome us. But that would be a backward step for people like us. We must do the best we can for ourselves and for those who follow us. Self-preservation is the first law of nature, you know."

Not just anyone would be invited to his ball. Only people who were up to proper standards would be asked. They would have to be of the right color and calling. His marriage to Mrs. Dixon would be an example for them all. It would further the social process he had been wishing and waiting for.

II

The ball was to take place on a Friday night. Everything in the house had been put in order. The carpets were covered with canvas. The halls and stairs were decorated with palms and potted plants. In the afternoon Mr. Ryder sat on his front porch reading Tennyson, his favorite poet. He was looking for the perfect lines to read at his ball. He wanted to express his admiration for Mrs. Dixon in the words of the poet.

Mr. Ryder heard the click of his gate latch. A light footstep sounded on the steps. When he looked up, he saw a woman standing at the porch steps.

She was a little woman, not five feet tall. She stood there, still and straight. She looked around with bright eyes. The woman must have been quite old. Her face was crossed and re-crossed with a hundred wrinkles. Tufts of short gray hair stuck out around the edges of her bonnet. She wore an old-fashioned blue dress and a red wool shawl.

The little woman was very black—so black that her toothless gums were not red, but blue. She looked like a bit of the old plantation life.

Mr. Ryder rose from his chair and came over to her.

"Good afternoon, madam," he said.

"Good evenin', suh," she answered, ducking in a curtsy. "Is dis here whar Mistuh Ryduh lib, suh?" she asked.

"Yes," he replied kindly. "I am Mr. Ryder. Did you want to see me?"

"Yas, suh, if I ain't disturbin' you."

"Not at all. Have a seat over here, where it is cool. What can I do for you?"

"'Scuse me, suh," she continued, sitting down on the edge of a chair. "'Scuse me.

I's lookin for my husban'. I heerd you was a big man and had libbed heah a long time. I hoped you wouldn't min' if I bothered you. Have you ever heerd of a light-colored man by de name of Sam Taylor? He might be coming round de churches, lookin' fer his wife Liza Jane."

Mr. Ryder stopped to think for a moment. There were many such cases right after the war. Slave families that had been separated came around looking for each other. "There are very few such questions asked now," he said. "But tell me your story. It may refresh my memory."

She folded her work-worn hands in her lap.

"My name's Liza," she began. "Liza Jane. When I was young I uster belong ter Marse Bob Smif. I was bawn down dere in old Missoura. When I was a gal I was married ter a man named Jim. But Jim died, and I married a light-colored man named Sam Taylor. Sam was free-bawn, but his mammy and daddy died.

Den de white folks sent him ter my marster. He was ter work for dem 'tel he was growed up. Sam worked in de fiel', and I was de cook. One day de old miss's maid came rushin' out ter de kitchen. 'Liza Jane,' says she, 'old marse gwine sell yo' Sam down de ribber.'

" 'But my husban's free!' says I.

"Don' make no difference. I heerd old marse tell old miss he was gwine take yo' Sam. He need de money, he said. And he knew whar he could git a thousan' dollars for Sam.'

"When Sam come home from de fiel' dat night, I told him 'bout old marse gwine steal him. Sam run erway. His time was most up. He swore dat when he was 21 he would come back and he'p me run erway, too. Or else he would save up de money and buy my freedom. And I know he'd of done it—fer he thought a heap of me! But when he came back he didn't find me, fer I wasn't dere. Old marse had heerd dat I warned Sam. So he had me whipped and sold me.

"Den de war broke out. When it was ober de cullud folks was scattered. I went back to de old home. But Sam wasn't dere, and I couldn't larn nuffin' 'bout him. I knowed he'd been dere ter look fer me and hadn't found me. Den he'd gone ter hunt fer me.

"I's been lookin' fer him eber sence," she added simply. "I know he's been lookin' fer me. I know he's been huntin' fer me all dese years. Unless he's sick or out'n his head, so he couldn't 'member his promise.

"I went back down de ribber. I figured he'd gone down dere lookin' fer me. I's been all der way ter Noo Orleens and Atlanty and Charleston and Richmon'. When I'd been all ober de Souf I come ter de Norf.

"I know I'll find him some of dese days. Or he'll find me," she added softly. "Den we'll bofe be as happy in freedom as we was in de old days before de war." Her bright eyes softened into a faraway look.

Mr. Ryder was looking at her curiously when she finished.

"How have you lived all these years?" he asked.

"Cookin', suh. I's a good cook. Does you know anybody what needs a good cook, suh? Just now I's stoppin' with a cullud family roun' de corner yonder."

"Do you really expect to find your husband? He may be dead long ago."

She shook her head. "Oh, no, he ain't dead. I dremp' three times dis week dat I foun' him."

"He may have married another woman," Mr. Ryder said. "Your slave marriage would not have prevented him. Since you never lived with him after the war, your marriage doesn't count."

"Dat wouldn't make no difference ter Sam. He wouldn't marry no other woman 'tel he found out 'bout me. I knows it," she added. "Sumpin's been tellin' me all dese years dat I's gwine find Sam 'fo I dies."

"Perhaps he's outgrown you. It may be that he's climbed up in the world. It may be that he wouldn't care to have you find him."

"No, indeed, suh," she replied. "Sam ain't dat kin' a man. He was good to me, Sam was."

"You may have already passed him on the street a hundred times," said Mr. Ryder. "After all, it's been 25 years! You may not have known him. Time works great changes."

She smiled. "I'd know him 'mongst a hundred men. Dey was no other man like my man Sam. I's toted his picture roun' with me all dis time."

"May I see it?" asked Mr. Ryder. "It might help me to remember if I've ever seen him."

She drew a small package from her dress. He saw that it was fastened to a string that went around her neck.

She removed several wrappers. Then she handed him an old-fashioned photo in a black case. He looked long and carefully at the picture. It was faded, but the features were still clear. It was easy to see what the man had looked like.

He closed the case and slowly handed it back to her.

"I don't know of any man in town who goes by that name," he said. "I haven't heard of anyone looking for you. But if you will leave me your address, I will give the matter some attention. If I find out anything I will let you know."

She gave him the number of a house in the neighborhood. After thanking him warmly, she went away.

He wrote the address in his book of poems. When she had gone, he rose to his feet and stood looking after her. He watched her turn the corner, and then went upstairs to his bedroom. For a long time he stood before the mirror and gazed at his own face.

III

At eight o'clock the ballroom was a blaze of light. The guests had begun to arrive. A black servant in evening dress directed the guests inside, where another servant took their coats.

The grand party was long remembered among the colored people of the city. It was not only remembered for the dress and display, but for the intelligence and culture among the guests. A number of school teachers had come, along with several young doctors, three or four lawyers, some singers, an editor, and an officer in the army. There were many others as well. All were colored, though many of them looked just like white people. Most of the ladies were in evening dresses. The men wore fine dress coats and elegant dancing shoes. A band played while the guests were gathering.

The dancing began at half past nine. At eleven o'clock supper was served. Mr. Ryder had left the ballroom some time before. But now he appeared at the supper table. The food was wonderful, and the guests ate with great enjoyment. When the coffee had been served, Mr. Sadler rapped for order. He made a brief speech. Then he presented the toasts of the evening.

The toastmaster reached the end of his list. "The last toast," he said, "will be to the ladies. Our host will do the honors."

With a thoughtful look, Mr. Ryder took the floor. He began by speaking of woman as heaven's gift to man. "Perhaps the most beautiful quality of woman is her devotion to those she loves," he said. "History is full of examples. But history has no more striking example than the one which came to my notice today."

Then his guests heard the story told by his afternoon visitor. He told the story in the same soft dialect, which came easily to his lips. All listened attentively. In many hearts, the story awoke a response.

"Such devotion and faith are rare even among women," Mr. Ryder went on. "There are many who would have searched a year. Some would have gone on for five years. Perhaps a few might have hoped for ten years. But for *25 years* this woman has kept her faith in one man. And she has not seen or heard of him in all that time.

"Today she came to me. She hoped that I could help her find this long-lost husband. And when she was gone, I imagined a case to myself. Tonight I will put this case to you.

"Suppose that this husband, soon after his escape, learned that his wife had been sold away. He could not find out anything about her. Suppose that he was young, and she was much older than he. Suppose that his skin was light, and her skin was black. Their marriage was a slave marriage. It was legal only if they chose to make it so after the war.

"Suppose, too, that he had made his way to the North. There he found opportunities, and made the most of them. In the course of all these years he had changed. Now he was far different from the ignorant boy who ran away. He was as different as day is from night. Suppose, even, that he had won the friendship of such fine people as I see around me tonight. I am old enough to remember when such a gathering as this would not have been possible!

"Let us suppose that this man's memory of the past had grown dim. Now it came back to him only in dreams. What would happen if chance brought him new knowledge? Suppose he discovered that the wife of his youth was alive and seeking him. My friends—what would the man do?

"I will say that this man was one who loved honor. He had tried all of his life to deal justly with people. I will even go further. Let us say that he had fallen in love with another. What would he do? Or, rather, what *should* he do—in such a crisis?

"It seemed to me that he might hesitate. I imagined that I was his old friend, and that he had come to me for advice. The two of us looked upon the matter from every point of view. Then I spoke to him. I used the well-known words of the poet:

'This above all: to thine own self
   be true,
And it must follow, as the night
   the day,
Thou canst not then be false to
   any man.'

"Then, finally, I put the question to him. 'Shall you acknowledge her?'

"And now, ladies and gentlemen, friends and companions, I ask *you*—What should he have done?"

Something in Mr. Ryder's voice stirred the hearts of those around him. They saw that this was no imaginary situation. It was more like a personal appeal. And the guests saw that Mr. Ryder's eyes rested upon Mrs. Dixon.

As she listened, her lips were parted and her eyes were streaming. She was the first to speak. "Of course he should have acknowledged her," she said.

"Yes," they all echoed. "He should have acknowledged her."

"My friends," responded Mr. Ryder, "I thank you all. It is the answer I expected—for I know your hearts."

Then he turned and walked toward a closed door. Every eye followed him. In a moment, he came back. He held the hand of his visitor of the afternoon. The tiny woman stood startled and trembling at the brilliant scene. Neatly dressed in gray, she wore the white cap of an old woman.

"Ladies and gentlemen," he said, "this is the woman, and I am the man, whose story I have told you. Permit me to introduce to you the wife of my youth."

A Matter of Principle

Is it possible to fight prejudice with prejudice? In this amusing story, a man's efforts to move up in the world have surprising results.

To Alice and her mother, the bold and flowery
letter was very exciting.

A Matter of Principle

Mr. Cicero Clayton was a well-respected man. At a meeting of the Blue Vein Society, he once made this statement: "In its treatment of the race problem, our country needs a clearer idea of the brotherhood of man."

Mr. Clayton had liked the sound of that statement. He had repeated it many times. He said it so often, in fact, that the younger members of the society got very tired of hearing it. Sometimes they spoke of him as "Brotherhood Clayton." In this way, they made fun of his strange idea.

The basis of Mr. Clayton's belief was that he himself was not a negro.

"I know," he would say, "that white people lump us all together as negroes. But I don't accept this classification myself. I also imagine that I have a right to my opinion. Some people—like myself—belong by half or more of their blood to the white race. Surely we have as much right to call ourselves white as others have to call us negroes."

Mr. Clayton spoke warmly, for he had thought much upon the subject.

Mr. Clayton lived up to his beliefs. He did this by avoiding unnecessary contact with black people. Every now and then this was a little inconvenient. Sometimes he and his family had to give up entertainments where many black people might be present. Instead, they mingled only with people like themselves.

Nearly all the members of their church were white. The Claytons also belonged to a number of organizations open to all good citizens. There they were treated with kindness and courtesy by the better class of white people.

Mr.Clayton had started out with a small amount of money left to him by his father. With this money he had started a restaurant. It had grown from a cheap eating-house into the most popular restaurant in Groveland. Now he owned houses and stores, and stocks and bonds. He lived in a grand style.

In person Mr. Clayton was of olive skin color, with slightly curly hair. He looked something like a Cuban or a Latin-American. Perhaps that is why he wore a pointed beard and a carefully waxed mustache. When he walked to church on Sundays with his daughter Alice on his arm, they made a striking couple.

Miss Alice Clayton was queen of her social set. She was young and pretty. She dressed in good taste. On top of that, her father was the richest colored man (which does not necessarily mean a negro) in Groveland.

Alice Clayton had only one social rival. That was Miss Lura Watkins. Miss

Watkins's father ran a successful business. His livery stable rented out the finest horses and carriages in town. Miss Lura Watkins's family lived in almost as fine style as the Claytons. Miss Watkins was also a good-looking young woman. But she was not quite so young nor quite so white as Miss Clayton. She was well-liked, however. The two young women were friends. There was a good-natured race between them to see which would make the first and best marriage.

Marriages in Miss Clayton's set were serious affairs. Their choices were very narrow. Miss Clayton and her friends would not marry black men. For the most part, white men would not marry them. So they had to choose among the young men of their own color. Sometimes the supply of eligible men ran short. When that happened, the girls in Miss Clayton's set went traveling.

Miss Clayton had more prospects than any of her friends. Her beauty and her position gave her first choice. Her father's wealth made her highly desirable. But for the same reason, she was more difficult to reach and harder to please. To get to her heart, a young man had to pass her parents' inspection. Until she had reached the age of 23 no young man had succeeded in doing this. Many had called, but none had been chosen.

Just one spot had been left unguarded. And Cupid, the ancient God of love, had already sent a dart through it. Mr. Clayton had taken into his household a poor cousin. This young boy—his name was Jack—had gone into Mr. Clayton's service at the age of 12 or 13.

At first Jack had helped with the housework. Meanwhile he attended school. Then his rich cousin had taken him into one of his stores.

Jack was grateful for what he could get—but he always meant to get more. By means of hard work and a pleasant manner, he got his employer to promote him. In time he had gained a good position in the business.

Anyone outside the family would have thought him a very suitable husband for Miss Clayton. He was the same age. He was as fair in color as she, and passably good-looking. He had a natural manliness.

Sometimes, when Miss Clayton had no other escort, Jack went out with her in the evening. But Mr. and Mrs. Clayton were accustomed to looking down on Jack. They could speak only jokingly of his prospects as a husband for their daughter.

"Well, Alice," her father would say, "you won't have to die as an old maid. If we can't find anything better for you, there's always Jack."

At first Miss Alice had not liked this joke. But over time she grew used to it. To Jack it was no joke at all. He had long wished for this marriage. In a casual way, he had even brought up the idea to Alice. She had treated the matter lightly. But he had hope that she was not displeased.

Then, Miss Clayton went away on a visit to Washington. There she attended a grand ball. Many important and successful young men were introduced to her. She danced until four o'clock in the morning. A day or two later she returned home. It had been the most delightful week of her life.

II

About three weeks after returning from Washington, Alice received a letter. On the envelope were the words "House of Representatives." The letter was from a congressman named Hamilton M. Brown. In it he reminded Miss Clayton of their meeting at the grand ball in Washington. He complimented her charm and beauty, and begged for a chance to see her again. He said that he would be visiting Groveland soon. He asked permission to call on her.

To Alice and her mother the bold and flowery letter was very exciting. They read it over again and again. A new suitor for Alice would be very acceptable. But the mere fact of his being a congressman was not enough to qualify him. There were other considerations.

"I've never heard of this Honorable Hamilton M. Brown," said Mr. Clayton. "It's strange, Alice, that you haven't said anything about him before. You must have met lots of important folks not to remember a congressman."

"But he wasn't a congressman then," answered Alice. "That was before the elections. I remember Senator Bruce, and Mr. Douglass. But there were dozens of doctors and lawyers and politicians. I couldn't keep track of them all. Still, I seem to have a faint memory of dancing with a Mr. Brown."

She brought out the dancing program that she had carried with her at the Washington ball.

"Yes," she said, "I see that I must have danced with him. Here are his initials—'H. M. B.'"

"What color is he?" asked Mr. Clayton.

"I have a notion that he was rather dark. Darker than anyone I had ever danced with before."

"Why did you dance with him, then?" asked her father. "You didn't have to forget your principles because you were away from home."

"Well, Father, Mrs. Clearweather introduced me to several dark men. They were her friends. Common decency required me to be polite."

"If this man is black, we don't want to encourage him. But if he's the right sort, we'll invite him to the house."

"And make him feel at home here," added Mrs. Clayton.

"We must ask Sadler about him tomorrow," said Mr. Clayton. "If he's the right man, he shall have a fine visit here indeed. We'll show him that Washington is not the only town on earth."

The family's questions about Mr. Brown were soon answered. Mr. Solomon Sadler dropped in after supper. Mr. Sadler knew the history of every important colored man in the country.

"Let me see," he said. "Yes, I think I know the Honorable Hamilton M. Brown. He studied at Oberlin just after the war. He was leaving there when I entered. As I remember, Hamilton was quite light. He was a very good-looking, gentlemanly fellow. And I heard that he was a good student and a fine speaker."

"Do you remember what kind of hair he had?" asked Mr. Clayton.

"Very good indeed. Straight, as I remember it. He looked something like a Spaniard or a Portuguese."

"Now that you describe him," said Alice, "I *do* remember dancing with such a gentleman. The dark man must have been someone else."

"I suppose this congressman will be all right, Alice," said her father when Sadler had left. "He seems to mean business, and we must treat him white. Of course he must stay with us. Let's see—he'll be here in three days. That isn't very long, but I guess we can get ready. I'll write a letter this evening. No, *you* write it—and invite him to the house. Say I'll meet him at the train station."

"We must invite some people to meet him," said Mrs. Clayton.

"Certainly. A big reception will be just the proper thing! Write the letter immediately. I'll mail it first thing in the morning. You and your mother can put your heads together and make out a list of guests. I'll have the invitations printed tomorrow. We'll show Groveland how to entertain a congressman!"

Alice wrote the letter on the spot. The next morning it was mailed and sped on its winged way to Washington.

III

On the evening of April 3rd, Mr. Clayton and Jack arrived at the Union Depot. Mr. Clayton looked at the blackboard on the station wall. He saw that the 7:30 train from Washington was running five minutes late. He and Jack walked up and down the platform until the train pulled in. Mr. Clayton stationed himself at the end gate.

"You'd better go and stand by the other gate, Jack," he said. "Stop him if he goes out that way."

A stream of passengers poured though. But Mr. Clayton saw no one who looked

like Sadler's description of Congressman
Brown. He wondered if his guest had
gone out by the other gate. Mr. Clayton
hurried there.

"Didn't he come out this way, Jack?"
he asked.

"No, sir," replied the young man. "I
haven't seen him."

"That's strange," mused Mr. Clayton.
"We'd better look around."

Mr. Clayton turned and walked along
the platform to the men's waiting room.
The only colored person in the room was
a very black man. He was wearing a suit
and a silk hat. Next to him stood two
suitcases. On one of them was written,
in large white letters:

H. M. Brown, M. C.
Washington, D.C.

Mr. Clayton's feelings at this sight can
hardly be described. He hastily left the
waiting room. The black gentleman was
looking the other way. He had not seen
Mr. Clayton at all. Now Mr. Clayton
walked rapidly up and down the

platform, wondering what to do. He had invited a light-colored man to his house. He had come down to meet, and planned to entertain, a light-colored man. By his theory, this was a white man—an acceptable guest, a possible husband for his daughter.

If the congressman had turned out to be brown—even dark brown, but with fairly good hair—Mr. Clayton could have welcomed him as a guest. He might not, however, have desired him as a son-in-law. But the man he saw in the waiting room was very, very black. He had woolly hair. He apparently had not a single drop of white blood.

How could Mr. Clayton go against his well-known principles? How could he take this negro into his home and introduce him to his friends? What a rude shock it would be to his wife and daughter. What a disappointment! The ghastly mistake was bad enough. But to have this black man come to his house would be twisting the arrow in the wound.

Mr. Clayton was a gentleman. He realized the delicacy of the situation. How could he get out of his difficulty without wounding the feelings of the congressman? Whatever he did must be done promptly. If he waited much longer the congressman would probably take a carriage to Mr. Clayton's house.

A ray of hope came. Perhaps the black man was merely sitting there. Perhaps he was not the owner of the suitcase. He was thinking over this possibility when Jack came running up to him.

"Jack!" he cried. "I'm afraid we're in the worst kind of a mess, unless there's some mistake! Run down to the men's waiting room. Find the black man with a suitcase. Ask him if he is the congressman from South Carolina. If he says yes, come back right away. Don't give him time to ask any questions."

"I wonder what's the matter?" said Jack to himself. But he did as he was told. In a moment he came running back.

"Yes, sir," he announced. "He says he's the man."

"Jack," said Mr. Clayton desperately, "you know how much I've done for you. Now I want you want to show your appreciation. You must think of some way out of this! I'd never dare to take that negro to my house. Yet I must treat the man like a gentleman."

Jack had a thoughtful look on his face. Suddenly his eyes brightened with understanding. As a newsboy ran into the station, he got an idea.

"*Clarion*, special edition!" shouted the newsboy. "Read about the epidemic of diphtheria!" As the newsboy walked into the waiting room, Jack darted after him. He saw the black man buy a paper. Then Jack hurried back to Mr. Clayton.

"I have it, sir!" he said. He seized a telegraph blank and wrote rapidly. "How's this for a way out?" He read aloud the note he had written.

DEAR SIR — An unfortunate event has interfered with our plans. My daughter Alice has developed a case of diphtheria. Our house has just been quarantined. I am sending this letter by messenger to protect you from infection. The messenger will drive you to the Forest Hill House. Please be my guest while you are at the hotel. I fear that no one of our family will be able to meet with you. We hope, however, that you may still enjoy your visit. There are many places of interest in the city. Many friends will be glad to meet you.

> *With profound regret, I am*
> *Sincerely yours,*
> *CICERO CLAYTON.*

"Splendid!" Mr. Clayton cried out. "You've helped me out of a horrible scrape. Now, for heaven's sake, take the man to the hotel. In another minute he'll be calling a carriage to drive to the house. I'll go home on a street car."

Mr. Clayton escaped from the station. "So far, so good," he sighed. "Jack is a clever fellow. I'll have to do something more for him. But the *real* tug-of-war is yet to come. I've got to bribe a doctor and shut up the house. Even worse, I'll have to put up with the ill-humor of two disappointed women. Well, I'm sure my wife and Alice will back me up. No sacrifice is too great to escape having to entertain him.

"Of course I have no prejudice against his color—he can't help that—it is just the *principle* of the thing. If we received him, it would be a fatal blow to all my beliefs and theories. And I am really doing him a kindness. I'm sure that nothing could make Alice and her mother treat him with anything but cold politeness. This will be a great hardship for Alice. But I don't see how else I could have taken care of it."

When he reached home, he went into the parlor. Closing the door, he told his story. After their first shock, the ladies agreed with him. He had done the only thing he could. Jack's quick thinking had saved the day. But, just as Mr. Clayton had predicted, Alice was very upset.

"So," said Mr. Clayton, "we've got to act quick. Alice must wrap up her throat. By the way, Alice, how *is* your throat feeling?"

"It's sore," sobbed Alice. The girl had been in tears almost since her father returned with the news. "I don't care if I *do* have diphtheria! I hope I die!" And she wept on.

"Wrap up your throat and go to bed. I'll go over to Dr. Pillsbury's and get a diphtheria card. We'll have to nail it up on the house. In the morning we'll write notes to call off the party. We'll have them delivered by messenger.

"Oh, we were fools not to find out about this man ourselves. Sadler doesn't know *half* he thinks he does! And we'll have to carry this thing off perfectly. Otherwise people will say that we are prejudiced. Of course, *we* know it is only a matter of principle with us."

The plan was carried out to the letter. The invitations were recalled. The family doctor came to the house several times. Alice remained in bed.

Mr. Clayton himself remained at home. About ten o'clock in the morning a letter came up from the hotel. It was a sympathy note from Mr. Brown. Toward noon Mr. Clayton picked up the morning paper. His eye fell on the headline, "A Colored Congressman."

The interview in the paper described the congressman as a tall and handsome man, about 35 years old. His olive skin was not noticeably darker than many a white man's, it said. His hair was straight and his eyes black.

The article went on, but the first part left Mr. Clayton shocked. The paper had fallen from his hand. What was the meaning of it? Had he been mistaken? Obviously so, or else the reporter was wrong. And that was not very likely.

When Mr. Clayton had recovered himself, he picked up the newspaper again. He began reading where he had left off.

"Representative Brown traveled to Groveland with Bishop Jones of the African Methodist Jerusalem Church.

Bishop Jones is on his way to attend a conference in Detroit. The Bishop is a splendid type of the pure negro. He is said to be a man of great power among his people."

Mr. Clayton stared at the paper. "'The bishop,' he repeated, "'is a splendid type of the pure negro.' I must have mistaken the bishop for the congressman! But how in the world did Jack get the thing messed up? I'll call him and demand an explanation.

"Jack," he said, "I want you to remember the fellow you gave the note to at the depot. What did he look like?"

"He was a very wicked-looking fellow, sir," Jack said seriously. "He had a bad eye. He looked like a gambler, sir. I'm not surprised that you didn't want to entertain him. Even if he was a congressman."

"What color was he? That's what I want to know. And what kind of hair did he have?"

"Why, he was about my color, sir. He had straight black hair."

The rules of the telephone company did not permit the kind of language Mr. Clayton then used.

"Was there anyone else with him?" he asked, when he had calmed down.

"Yes, sir. Bishop Jones of the African Methodist Jerusalem Church was sitting there with him. They had traveled from Washington together. I drove the bishop to his stopping-place after I left Mr. Brown at the hotel. I didn't suppose you'd mind."

Mr. Clayton fell into a chair. He gave in to unspeakable thoughts.

"I'll hide the paper, anyway," he groaned. "I'll never hear the last of this till my dying day. Such bad luck! It's enough to disgust a man! I was only trying to do right and live up to my principles!"

Time hung heavy on Mr. Clayton's hands that day. He answered several telephone calls about Alice's health. After lunch he took a nap on the sofa. He was awakened when he heard the evening paper being dropped on the front porch.

Quickly Mr. Clayton looked to see if there was any more news of the visiting congressman. He found the article at once.

"The congressman will be the guest of Mr. William Watkins," the article said. "Mr. Watkins is the owner of the popular livery stable on Main Street. Mr. Brown will stay in the city for several days. On Wednesday evening there will be a reception for him at Mr. Watkins's."

"That ends it," sighed Mr. Clayton. "The dove of peace will never again rest on my roof."

But why dwell any longer on the sufferings of Mr. Clayton? Why try to describe the feelings of his wife and daughter? Why report the remarks they made when they learned the facts of the case?

Representative Brown was given a warm welcome in the home of Mr. William Watkins. At the brilliant party on Wednesday evening, Mr. Brown took a fancy to Miss Lura Watkins. Before the week was over, the two of them were engaged to be married. In the meantime, poor Alice lay sick in bed. A victim of principles, she had a fake case of diphtheria and a real case of terrible disappointment.

A few weeks later, Alice and Jack were on the way home from evening church. "What a dreadful thing it all was!" Alice was saying. "And to think of that hateful Lura Watkins marrying the congressman!"

The street was shaded by trees, and there was no one in sight. Jack put his arm around her waist. Leaning over, he kissed her.

"Never mind, dear," he said. "You still have your 'last chance' left. I'll prove myself better than the congressman."

Nothing has changed at the social meetings of the Blue Veins. The future of the colored race still comes up for discussion. And Mr. Clayton still makes his famous remark.

"The white people of the United States need a higher concept of the brotherhood of man," he says. "For of one blood God made all the nations of the earth."

The Sheriff's Children

Is it ever too late to right an old wrong? In this dramatic story, a lawman is forced to face a present challenge and a past regret.

"KEEP BACK FROM THE WINDOW. IF THEY SEE YOU THEY MIGHT SHOOT."

The Sheriff's Children

A murder was a rare event in Branson County. So there was great excitement when the news reached Troy early one Friday morning. Old Captain Walker had been murdered! Business nearly stopped. All over town people gathered in little groups to talk about the crime.

Who could the killer be? Some facts had already come out. Someone had seen a strange, light-skinned negro walking by Captain Walker's house the night before. Someone else had passed the same man leaving Troy early

Friday morning. Early that evening, the sheriff's posse had found him. The suspect was taken to the county jail.

The murder was all that people could talk about. At the house of mourning, a steady stream of visitors paid their last respects. They gazed upon the rugged face of the old soldier, now stiff and cold in death. More than one eye dropped a tear at the memory of his cheery smile. Anger boiled up among the crowd. They began to feel that ordinary justice was too mild a punishment for such a crime.

Toward noon a small crowd had gathered in Dan Tyson's store. For an hour or two the men muttered to each other and drank a great deal of moonshine whiskey. At last they decided to lynch the negro. They agreed that this was the least they could do. What else would avenge the death of their murdered friend?

In ordinary times these were not bad people. They had some notion of the power of the law and the rights of all citizens. But in the passion of the moment, all of this was forgotten. *A white man had been killed by a negro.*

The lynchers planned to come back to Tyson's store at five o'clock that afternoon. Then they would go straight to the jail, about a half mile away.

It was twenty minutes to five when Sheriff Campbell heard knocking. An excited negro had rushed up to the back door of the Campbells' house. When the man caught his breath, he warned the sheriff about the lynching party. He said that he had overheard the drunken men talking at the store.

The sheriff listened calmly. But as he heard the story out, his mouth set in a firm line. A determined gleam lit up his gray eyes. He looked like a soldier getting ready to meet the enemy.

"Much obliged, Sam," he said. "I'll protect the prisoner. Who's coming?"

"I dunno who all is comin'," replied Sam. "Dere's Mistah McSwayne, and Doc Cain, and Major McDonald, and Colonel Wright, and a heap a' others. I was so skeered I done forgot mo' den half of 'em.

I 'spec dey mus' be 'mos here by dis time, so I'll get outen de way. I don' want nobody ter think I was mixed up in dis business."

With that, the negro hurried off. The sheriff put on his coat and hat. Then he took down a double-barreled shotgun and loaded it with buckshot. Next he brought out a revolver. He filled the chambers with bullets. Then he slipped the gun into his coat pocket.

A handsome young woman had just come into the room. She wore a look of surprise on her face.

"Where are you going, Father?" she asked. She had not heard him talking with Sam.

"I've got to get over to the jail," the sheriff answered. "There's a mob coming this way to lynch the man we've got locked up. But they won't do it," he added.

"Oh, Father! Don't go!" pleaded the young woman. "They'll shoot you if you don't give him up to them."

"You never mind about me, Polly," said her father. "I'll take care of myself—and the prisoner, too. There ain't a man in Branson County that would shoot me. Besides, I've faced fire too often to be scared away from my duty. You keep close in the house," he warned her. "If anyone disturbs you, just use the old horse-pistol."

Branson's sheriff was far above the average man in the community. He had wealth, education, and social position. Before the Civil War, his family had owned more land and more slaves than any in the county. He had served with great bravery in the Confederate army. After the war, he was easily elected to the office of sheriff. No one had run against him. By now he had filled the office for several terms. Everyone in the county thought highly of him.

Sheriff Campbell had a strong sense of responsibility for his office. He had sworn to do his duty faithfully. And he understood very clearly what his duty as sheriff was. Perhaps this duty was clearer to him than any other.

The sheriff had just locked the heavy front door of the jail behind him. It was then that he heard them coming. He turned and saw a half dozen horsemen, followed by a crowd of men on foot. They were coming around a bend in the road. Now they halted in front of the sheriff's house. One of them dismounted and rapped on the door.

"Is the sheriff at home?" the man asked.

"No, he's just gone out," said Polly.

"We've come for the jail keys," the man insisted.

"They are not here," said Polly. "The sheriff took them with him. He is at the jail now."

The man returned to his friends and told them what she had said. They guessed that the sheriff had learned of their plan. He must be preparing to resist it.

Then one of the men rapped on the jailhouse door.

"Well, what is it?" the sheriff called out.

"We want to talk to you, Sheriff," replied the spokesman.

"All right, boys, talk away," the sheriff said without opening the door. "What business do you have here?"

"We're tax-payin' citizens," the man said. "And we want to get into the jail."

"What for? It ain't hard to get *into* jail. Most people want to keep *out*!"

No one laughed at the sheriff's joke.

"We want to have a talk with Cap'n Walker's killer."

"You can talk to the prisoner in the courthouse. He'll be brought out for trial next week."

"If yer don't let us in," cried a voice, "we'll bust the door down."

"Bust away," answered the sheriff. "But I warn you. The first man that tries it will be filled with buckshot. I'm sheriff of this county. I know my duty, and I mean to do it."

The crowd drew off a little. The leaders talked together in low tones.

The Branson County jail was a small two-story building. There were never many prisoners in it, so the lower windows had been boarded up. Now the sheriff climbed to the second floor. There was just one place up there to look out. That was the window of the prisoner's cell. The sheriff unlocked the door and entered the cell. He saw that the prisoner was crouched in a corner. His teeth were chattering with fright.

"For God's sake, Sheriff," the young man murmured, "don't let 'em lynch me. I didn't kill the old man."

"Get up," the sheriff said. He felt disgust for the man's cowardice. "You will probably be hung sooner or later. But it shall not be today, if I can help it. I'll unlock your irons. If I can't hold the jail, you'll have to make the best fight you can. If I'm shot, I consider my responsibility at an end."

The sheriff unlocked the prisoner's leg irons and handcuffs. They fell clanking to the floor.

"Keep back from the window," said the sheriff. "If they see you they might shoot."

The sheriff laid his revolver on a bench. Then he took up his rifle and stood a little back from the window.

The lynchers were not prepared to fight a battle. No one wanted to attack the jail. Finally one of them spoke to the others.

"Well, boys," the man said, "we'll have to let it go for now. The sheriff says he'll shoot. There ain't any of us that want to follow Cap'n Walker jest yet. Besides, the sheriff is a good fellow. We don't want to hurt him."

There was a murmur from the mob. Several voices shouted out that an attack must be made. But finally, with much grumbling, they headed for home.

The sheriff stood at the window until they rode off. But he did not relax until the last one was out of sight. That is why he neither saw nor heard the prisoner creeping across the floor. While the sheriff looked out the window, the prisoner grabbed the revolver from the bench. Then he crept quietly back to his place in the corner.

Suddenly a shot was fired from the woods across the road. The sheriff fired twice in the direction of the shot. Then he reached behind him for the other weapon. It was not on the bench! As the sheriff turned his head, he looked into the muzzle of the revolver.

"Stay where you are, Sheriff," said the prisoner.

The sheriff was a brave man, but he was no fool. It was clear to him that the prisoner was now in charge. The two men stood still for a moment. They fought a harmless battle with their eyes.

"Well, what do you mean to do?" asked the sheriff.

"To get away, of course," said the prisoner. His tone made the sheriff look at him more closely. This keen-eyed, desperate man was nothing like the whining wretch who had begged for his life a few minutes before.

Now the sheriff looked for a chance to turn the tables on him. After a moment he spoke.

"Is this your gratitude to me? Don't you know that I saved your life at the risk of my own? If I had not done so, you would be swinging from the limb of a tree right now."

"True," said the prisoner. "You saved my life. But for how long? When you came in, you said court would be next week. When the crowd went away, they said I had not long to live. It is only the choice of two ropes."

"If you are innocent you can prove it in court," the sheriff said.

"I didn't kill the old man," the prisoner said. "But I would never be able to clear myself. I was at his house at nine o'clock. I stole a coat there. That coat was on my back when I was taken. Even with a fair trial, I would be convicted. Unless the real murderer is caught, you know I have no chance."

The sheriff knew this only too well. He tried to think of another argument. The

prisoner went on, "Throw me the keys—
no, unlock the door."

The sheriff crossed the room and
unlocked the door.

"Now go down and unlock the outside
door."

The sheriff's heart leaped in his chest.
Perhaps he could make a run for it! He
walked down the stairs with the prisoner
close behind him.

The sheriff pushed the huge iron key
into the lock. The rusty bolt yielded
slowly. He thought about dashing out
the door.

"Stop!" thundered the prisoner. "Move
a muscle, and I'll blow your brains out."

The sheriff obeyed.

"Now stay close to the wall. Go back
upstairs."

When they reached the cell, the sheriff
expected the man to lock him up and
make his own escape. He decided to go
along with whatever the prisoner said.
He would try to recapture the man
later—after the alarm had been given.

More than once the sheriff had faced death on the battlefield. A few minutes before, he had been well armed. With a brick wall between him and the mob, he had dared a hundred men to fight. But now he felt the desperation of the man confronting him. The sheriff was too prudent to risk his life against such heavy odds. There was Polly to think of.

"I just want to get away," said the prisoner. "If I'm captured, I know they will hang me on the spot. But in order to save myself, I may have to kill you."

"Good God!" cried the sheriff. "You would not kill the man to whom you owe your own life!"

"You speak more truly than you know," replied the light-skinned man. "I indeed owe my life to you."

The sheriff started. "Who are you?" he asked in amazement.

"Tom—Cicely's son," returned the other. He had closed the cell door. Now he stood talking to the sheriff through the small grated opening. "Don't you remember Cicely? Cicely, whom you sold—along with her child?"

The sheriff did remember. He had been sorry for it ever since. It had been the old story of debts, mortgages, and bad crops. He had quarreled with Cicely. The price offered for her had been very large. He had given in to anger and need.

"Good God!" he gasped. "You would not murder your own father?"

"My *father*?" replied the prisoner. "It would be one thing for *me* to claim the relationship. But it comes with poor grace from you! How dare you ask anything for that reason! What father's duty did you ever perform for me? Did you give me your name, or even your protection? Other white men gave their colored sons freedom and money. They sent them to the free states. *You* sold *me* to the rice swamps."

"I at least gave you the life you cling to," murmured the sheriff.

"Life? What kind of a life? You gave me your blood and your spirit. But then you made me a slave, and you crushed it out."

"But you are free now," said the sheriff.

"Free to do what?"

"There are schools. You have been to school." He had noticed that the prisoner used better language than most Branson County people.

"I have been to school. It was there that I discovered that no amount of learning will change the color of my skin. I do not care for a degraded life. It is the animal in me, not the man, that flees the gallows. Will you promise to give no alarm if I do not shoot you?"

The sheriff hesitated.

"Stop," said the prisoner, "you need not promise. I could not trust you if you did. There is but one safe way for me. You must die."

Just as he raised his arm to fire, there was a bright flash. A gunshot rang from the hallway behind him. His arm fell to his side, and the pistol at his feet.

The sheriff threw open the door and grabbed the fallen weapon. Then he threw the prisoner into the cell. After locking the door, he turned to his rescuer.

His daughter Polly leaned, half-fainting, against the wall.

"Oh, Father, I was just in time!" she cried. Sobbing, she threw herself into her father's arms.

"I heard the shot from the woods. I saw you shoot back. When you didn't come out, I feared that something had happened. I got the other pistol and ran over here. I was just in time to hear him say he would kill you. Oh, it was a narrow escape!"

After Polly had calmed down, they bound up the prisoner's wound. Now there was no sign in his face of fear or disappointment. He showed no feeling of any kind.

"I'll have a doctor come by in the morning and dress the wound," the sheriff said to the prisoner. "If you will keep quiet, it will do very well until then. Tell the doctor that you were struck by the bullet fired from the woods."

The prisoner did not answer. He turned away from them. Polly and her father returned to the house.

That night the sheriff could not sleep. A flood of thoughts churned in his mind. He saw that he had owed some duty to this son of his. He saw that neither law nor custom could destroy such a responsibility. As these thoughts became clear to him, his anger against the young man died away. In its place there sprang up a great pity.

A caring father might have saved this boy's fiery spirit. He could have sent the boy to the free North. He could have given him an opportunity to use his talents. There were many things he could have done—but he had not done any of them.

The sheriff recalled his own youth. He had inherited an honored name. He had been helped to make a future. A fair young bride had beckoned him on to happiness. Then he thought about the poor wretch lying on a pallet of straw in the jail. He had had none of these things.

The sheriff began to think about what he still could do. He could move heaven and earth to discover the real killer. He could find a lawyer to help him. Perhaps the prisoner would be proved not guilty. Hope rose up in the sheriff's heart. Perhaps he could find a way to make up for his crime against this son of his—against society—against God.

With this decision the sheriff fell into a restless sleep. He awoke late the next morning.

He went to the jail before breakfast and found the prisoner lying on his pallet. His face was turned to the wall. He did not move when the sheriff rattled the door.

The sheriff quickly unlocked the door. He rushed into the cell and bent over the motionless form. There was no sound of breathing. He turned the body over—it was cold and stiff. The prisoner had torn the bandage from his wound and bled to death during the night. It appeared that he had been dead for several hours.

Thinking About the Stories

The Wife of His Youth

1. Who is the main character in this story? Who are one or two of the minor characters? Describe each of these characters in one or two sentences.

2. Interesting story plots often have unexpected twists and turns. What surprises did you find in this story?

3. Good writing always has an effect on the reader. How did you feel when you finished reading this story? Were you surprised, horrified, amused, sad, touched, or inspired? What elements in the story made you feel that way?

A Matter of Principle

1. All the events in a story are arranged in a certain order, or sequence. Tell about one event from the beginning of this story, one from the middle, and one from the end. How are these events related?

2. Did the story plot change direction at any point? Explain the turning point of the story.

3. What is the title of this story? Can you think of another good title?

The Sheriff's Children

1. Compare and contrast at least two characters in this story. In what ways are they alike? In what ways are they different?

2. An author builds the plot around the conflict in a story. In this story, what forces or characters are struggling against each other? How is the conflict finally resolved?

3. Suppose this story had a completely different outcome. Can you think of another effective ending for this story?

LAKE CLASSICS

Great American Short Stories I

Washington Irving, Nathaniel Hawthorne, Mark Twain, Bret
Harte, Edgar Allan Poe, Kate Chopin, Willa Cather, Sarah
Orne Jewett, Sherwood Anderson, Charles W. Chesnutt

Great American Short Stories II

Herman Melville, Stephen Crane, Ambrose Bierce, Jack
London, Edith Wharton, Charlotte Perkins Gilman, Frank R.
Stockton, Hamlin Garland, O. Henry, Richard Harding Davis

Great British and Irish Short Stories

Arthur Conan Doyle, Saki (H. H. Munro), Rudyard Kipling,
Katherine Mansfield, Thomas Hardy, E. M. Forster, Robert
Louis Stevenson, H. G. Wells, John Galsworthy, James Joyce

Great Short Stories from Around the World

Guy de Maupassant, Anton Chekhov, Leo Tolstoy, Selma
Lagerlöf, Alphonse Daudet, Mori Ogwai, Leopoldo Alas,
Rabindranath Tagore, Fyodor Dostoevsky, Honoré de Balzac

Cover and Text Designer: Diann Abbott

Library of Congress Catalog Number: 94-075021
ISBN 1-56103-011-2
Printed in the United States of America
1 9 8 7 6 5 4 3 2 1

LAKE CLASSICS

*Great American
Short Stories I*

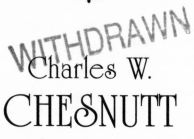

Charles W.
CHESNUTT

Stories retold by C.D. Buchanan
Illustrated by James Balkovek

LAKE EDUCATION
Belmont, California

🌿 Lake Classic Short Stories 🌿

*"The universe is made of
stories, not atoms."*
—Muriel Rukeyser

"The story's about you."
—Horace

Everyone loves a good story. It is hard
to think of a friendlier introduction to
classic literature. For one thing, short
stories are *short*—quick to get into and
easy to finish. Of all the literary forms,
the short story is the least intimidating
and the most approachable.

Great literature is an important part
of our human heritage. In the belief that
this heritage belongs to everyone, *Lake
Classic Short Stories* are adapted for
today's readers. Lengthy sentences and
paragraphs are shortened. Archaic words
are replaced. Modern punctuation and
spellings are used. Many of the longer
stories are abridged. In all the stories,

painstaking care has been taken to preserve the author's unique voice.

Lake Classic Short Stories have something for everyone. The hundreds of stories in the collection cover a broad terrain of themes, story types, and styles. Literary merit was a deciding factor in story selection. But no story was included unless it was as enjoyable as it was instructive. And special priority was given to stories that shine light on the human condition.

Each book in the *Lake Classic Short Stories* is devoted to the work of a single author. Little-known stories of merit are included with famous old favorites. Taken as a whole, the collected authors and stories make up a rich and diverse sampler of the story-teller's art.

Lake Classic Short Stories guarantee a great reading experience. Readers who look for common interests, concerns, and experiences are sure to find them. Readers who bring their own gifts of perception and appreciation to the stories will be doubly rewarded.

❦ Stephen Crane ❧
(1871–1900)

About the Author

Born in the city of Newark, New Jersey, Stephen Crane was the 14th and youngest child in his family. As the son of a Methodist minister, he grew up in full rebellion against the strictness of his family. He loved everything that his father and mother disapproved of— baseball, the theater, and novels.

Crane wrote his first novel, *Maggie: A Girl of the Streets*, when he was only 20 years old. He wrote it in a fraternity house during the only year he spent in college. He had to borrow money to get it typed, and then he went on to publish it at his own expense.

The Red Badge of Courage was published when Crane was just 24. It is the story of a young soldier's experience in the Civil War. He called this book a "psychological study of fear." When it came out, *The Red Badge of Courage* established his reputation. It is still his best-known work.

Crane spent some time writing for newspapers. *The Open Boat* was written after Crane himself was shipwrecked in January 1897. Sent to report on the Cuban Revolution, Crane boarded a steamer loaded with supplies for the Cuban rebels. Later, when the ship sank, Crane was reported killed. His impressions of that terrifying experience at sea are recorded in this story.

Crane died of tuberculosis when he was only 29. In his short life, he gave the world some great stories about brave characters who are struggling with overpowering forces. If you find it interesting to watch the human mind dealing with stress, Stephen Crane's stories are for you.

The Open Boat

Sometimes authors weave a story around an event that really happened. This gripping adventure is based on the author's own experience. Can you imagine what it would be like to be stranded at sea? In this story, you will share the hopes and fears of four men as they desperately try to reach land.

"I WISH WE HAD A SAIL," THE CAPTAIN SAID. "WE MIGHT TRY MY OVERCOAT ON THE END OF AN OAR."

The Open Boat

The Experience of Four Men from the
Sunk Steamer Commodore

I

None of them knew the color of the sky. Their eyes looked straight ahead at the waves that swept toward them. Except for their foaming white tops, the waves were gray. All around them the horizon narrowed and widened, dipped and rose. And at all times the horizon's edge was jagged with waves that seemed to have points like rocks.

Many men had bathtubs larger than the boat which here rode upon the sea.

It was only a ten-foot dinghy—nothing more than a rowboat. Each wave that hit the little boat was a dangerous problem. Squatting in the bottom, the cook was trying to bail out the boat. His eyes were set on the six inches of the boat's edge that separated him from the ocean. His sleeves were rolled over his fat forearms. As he bailed, the two flaps of his vest dangled and flapped.

The oiler was steering with one of the boat's two oars. It was a thin little oar, and it often seemed ready to snap. When water swirled in over the stern, the oiler would quickly stand up to keep clear of the downpour.

The journalist pulled at the other oar. He watched the waves and wondered why he was there.

The injured captain was lying in the bow of the boat. He seemed buried in a deep sadness. Strangely, he felt almost a lack of interest in the situation. This feeling comes even to the bravest and most strong-willed of men. It comes when—in a snap of the fingers—the company fails, or the army loses. Or in this case, when a man's ship goes down. When the captain spoke, there was something strange in his voice. It was steady—but it was deep with mourning, and sad beyond tears.

"Keep her a little more south, Billie," the captain said.

"A little more south, sir," the oiler in the stern said.

A seat in this boat was something like a seat on a bucking bronco. And by the same token, a bronco is not much smaller. The boat pranced and reared and plunged like an animal. As each wave came, she rose to meet it, like a horse jumping a very high fence.

There is one big disadvantage about the sea. You may successfully fight off *one* wave—but then you see that there is another one right behind it. And that second wave is just as determined to swamp a boat as is the first one. Now, as each wall of water approached the boat, it shut out all else from the men's view. It was easy to imagine that this very wave was the last and final outburst of the ocean. But it never was.

The sun swung steadily up in the sky. The men knew it was broad day because the color of the sea had changed from gray to emerald-green. And the foam of the waves was like tumbling snow. They had not watched the sun rising in the sky to bring the breaking day. They were only aware of the sun's effect on the color of the waves that rolled toward them.

The cook and the journalist were now having an argument. They were arguing over the difference between a life-saving station and a house of refuge.

The cook said, "There's a house of refuge just north of the Mosquito Inlet

Light. As soon as they see us, they'll come out in their boat and pick us up."

"As soon as *who* see us?" said the journalist.

"The crew," said the cook.

"Houses of refuge don't *have* crews," said the journalist. "Those places store clothes and food for shipwrecked people. They don't carry crews."

"Oh, yes, they do," said the cook.

"No, they don't," said the journalist.

"Well, we're not there yet, anyhow," said the oiler from his place in the stern.

"Well," said the cook, "perhaps it's not a house of refuge that I'm thinking of. Perhaps it's a life-saving station."

"We're not there yet," said the oiler.

II

"Good thing it's an on-shore wind," said the cook. "If not, where would we be? We wouldn't have a show."

"That's right," the journalist said.

The busy oiler nodded his head in agreement. Then the captain, lying in the bow, laughed in a way that expressed humor, scorn, and tragedy all in one. "Do you think we have much of a show now, boys?" he asked.

The other three were silent. They felt it was silly to express much optimism at this time. After all, they were miles from shore. And their small boat was being constantly pounded by waves. On the other hand, because of that very position, it didn't seem to be a good idea to express hopelessness either. So they were silent.

"Oh, well, we'll get ashore all right," said the captain.

But there was a certain tone in his voice that made them think. So the oiler said, "Yes! If this wind holds."

The cook was bailing. "Yes! If we don't catch hell in the surf."

All the while, the oiler and the journalist rowed and rowed. They sat together in the same seat, each rowing his oar. Then the oiler took both oars. Then the journalist took both oars. Then the oiler, then the journalist. They rowed and they rowed.

The tricky part came when it was time for another man to take his turn at the oars. It is easier to steal eggs from under a hen than it was to change seats in that boat. As the two men carefully changed places, the whole party kept watchful eyes on the coming wave. And the captain cried out, "Look out, now! Steady there!"

After a while, the boat soared on a great swell. The captain reared upward in the bow. He said that he had seen the lighthouse at Mosquito Inlet. A moment later, the cook said that he had seen it also.

The journalist was at the oars then. He, too, wanted to see the lighthouse, but his back was toward the far shore. And fighting the waves was more important.

For some time he could not get a chance to turn his head. Then a wave came that seemed more gentle than the others. The journalist quickly glanced at the western horizon.

"See it?" said the captain.

"No," said the journalist. "I didn't see anything."

"Look again," said the captain. He pointed. "It's exactly in that direction."

At the top of another big wave, the journalist did as he was told. This time his eyes focused on a small, still thing in the distance. It looked like the point of a pin. It took an anxious eye to find a lighthouse so tiny.

"Think we'll make it, Captain?" the journalist asked.

"If the wind holds, and this boat don't swamp, we can't do much else," the captain said.

"Keep bailing her, cook," said the captain calmly.

"All right, Captain," the cheerful cook said.

III

It would be hard to describe the brotherhood the men established on the high seas. No one said that it was so. No one talked about it. But it lived in the boat, and each man felt it warm him. They were a captain, an oiler, a cook, and a journalist. And they were friends. They were friends in a curious, iron-bound way.

The injured captain always spoke in a low and calm voice. But he could never command a more obedient crew than those three in the boat. What moved them was more than concern for their common safety. There was a quality among them that was personal and heartfelt.

After their devotion to the commander of the boat, there was comradeship among all of them. The journalist, for instance, had always been taught to be suspicious of people. Yet he knew, even at the time, that this was the best experience of his life. But no one said aloud that it was so. No one mentioned it.

"I wish we had a sail," the captain said. "We might try my overcoat on the end of an oar. It would give you two boys a chance to rest."

So the cook and the journalist held the mast and spread the overcoat wide. The oiler steered, and the little boat made good time with her new rig.

Meanwhile the lighthouse was slowly growing larger. It had almost taken on color. It looked like a little gray shadow on the horizon. The man at the oars couldn't help but turn his head often to get a look at this little gray shadow.

At last, from the top of each wave, the men in the tossing boat could see land.

"We must be opposite New Smyrna," said the cook. He had often coasted that part of the Florida shore in schooners. "By the way, Captain," he said, "I believe they shut down the life-saving station there a year ago."

"Did they?" the captain said.

The wind slowly died away. The cook and the journalist no longer worked so hard to hold the oar high. But the waves continued to swoop at the boat. No longer pushed by the wind, the little craft struggled against them. Then the oiler or the journalist took the oars again.

Shipwrecks can come quickly out of nowhere. If men could only train for them and have them occur when they are in top condition! Then there would be less drowning at sea. None of the men in the boat had slept for two days and two nights. To make matters worse, they had also forgotten to eat much before abandoning the steamer. For these reasons and more, neither the oiler nor the journalist was fond of rowing at this time.

"Take her easy, now, boys," the captain said. "Don't spend yourselves. If we have to run a surf, you'll need all your strength. Then for sure we'll have to swim for it. Take your time."

Slowly the land rose from the sea. From one black line it became a line of black and a line of white—trees and sand. Finally the captain said that he could make out a house on the shore.

"That's the house of refuge for sure," said the cook. "They'll see us before long and come out after us."

The distant lighthouse reared high. "The keeper should be able to make us out now, if he's looking through a glass," said the captain. "He'll tell the life-saving people."

"None of those other boats could have gotten ashore," said the oiler in a low voice. "No one will have had word of the wreck. Otherwise, the lifeboat would be out looking for us."

The wind came again. Then a new sound struck the ears of the men in the boat. It was the low thunder of the surf on the shore.

"We'll never be able to make the lighthouse now," said the captain. "Swing her a little more north, Billie."

"A little more north, sir," said the oiler.

So the little boat turned her nose once more down the wind. And all but the oarsman watched as the shore came nearer. It would still be tricky to manage the boat in these waters. But the sight of land so close made them quietly cheerful. In an hour, perhaps, they would be ashore.

IV

"Cook, there doesn't seem to be any sign of life in your house of refuge," the captain said.

"No," replied the cook. "Funny they don't see us!"

Tide, wind, and waves were swinging the boat northward.

"Funny they don't see us," said the men.

The surf's roar was duller now, but its tone was still thunderous and mighty. As the boat swam over the great waves, the men sat listening to this roar. "We'll swamp for sure," they said to each other.

It is fair to say here that there wasn't a life-saving station within 20 miles in either direction. But the men did not know this. So they made dark and nasty comments about the eyesight of the nation's life-savers. Four angry men sat in the boat and cursed their bad luck. Within eyesight was the shore of a land full of people. It made them bitter to see no sign of rescue coming from it.

"Well, I suppose we'll have to make a try for ourselves," the captain said at last. "If we stay out here too long, none of us will have the strength to swim, after the boat swamps."

So the oiler, who was at the oars, turned the boat straight for the shore.

"If we don't all get ashore—I suppose you fellows know where to send news of my finish?" said the captain. So the group quickly exchanged addresses and final messages to loved ones.

As for the thoughts of the men, there was a great deal of rage in them. Perhaps they were thinking this way: "If I am going to be drowned—why now? In the name of the mad gods who rule the sea, why was I allowed to come far enough to see sand and trees? Was I brought here just to have my nose dragged away as I was about to nibble the cheese of life? If Fate cannot do better than this, she should not be allowed to manage men's fortunes.

"If Fate has decided to drown me, why didn't she do it in the beginning? She would have saved me all this trouble. The whole thing is ridiculous. But no, she cannot mean to drown me. She *dare not* drown me. Not after all this work."

The waves that came now were stronger than before. They seemed always just about to roll the boat over in a mass of foam. And the shore was still a way off.

"Boys, she won't last three minutes more," said the oiler at the oars. "And we're too far out to swim. Shall I take her to sea again, Captain?"

"Yes, go ahead!" the captain said.

Then the oiler used a series of fast and steady oarsmanship moves. He turned the boat in the middle of the surf and took her safely out to sea again.

"What do you think of those life-saving people?" someone finally said. "Aren't they something?"

"Maybe they think we're out here for sport!" someone else answered. "Maybe they think we're fishin'. Maybe they think we're damned fools."

It was a long afternoon. A changed tide tried to force them southward. But the wind and waves pushed them northward. Far ahead there were little dots that seemed to suggest a city on the shore.

"St. Augustine?" someone asked.

The captain shook his head. "No. Too near Mosquito Inlet."

"Look! There's a man on the shore!"

"Where?"

"There! See him? See him?"

"Yes, sure! He's walking along."

"Now he's stopped. Look! He's facing our direction!"

"He's waving at us!"

"So he is! By thunder!"

"Ah, now we're all right! Now we're all right! There will be a boat out here for us in half an hour."

"He's going on. He's running. He's going up to that house there."

The captain saw a floating stick, and they rowed toward it. By some odd chance a bath towel was in the boat. Now they tied it to the stick, and the captain waved the makeshift flag. The oarsman did not dare turn his head. So he had to ask questions.

"What's he doing now?"

"He's standing still again. He's looking. I think... There he goes again—toward the house. Now he's stopped again."

"Is he waving at us?"

"No, not now. He *was*, though."

"Look! There comes another man!"

"He's running."

"Look at him go, would you!"

"Why, he's on a bicycle. Now he's met the other man. They're both waving at us. Look!"

"There comes something up the beach."

"What the devil is that thing?"

"Why, it looks like a boat."

"Why, certainly it's a boat!"

"No, it's on wheels."

"Yes, so it is. Well, that must be the lifeboat. They drag them along shore on a wagon."

"That's the lifeboat, sure."

"It is not! It's a bus. I can see it plain. See? It's one of those big hotel buses."

"By thunder, you're right. It's a bus, sure as fate. What do you suppose they are doing with a bus? Maybe they are going around collecting the life-crew, hey?"

"That's it, likely. Look! There's a fellow waving a little black flag. He's standing on the steps of the bus. There come those other two fellows. Now they're talking together. Look at the fellow with the flag. Maybe he *isn't* waving it!"

"That's not a flag, is it? That's his coat."

"So it is. It's his coat. He's taken it off and he's waving it around his head. Look at him swing it!"

"Say, there isn't any life-saving station there. That's just a winter-resort hotel bus. It's probably brought over some of the guests to see us drown."

"What's that idiot with the coat doing? What's he signaling, anyway?"

"It looks like he's trying to tell us to go north. There must be a life-saving station up there."

"No, he thinks we're fishing. Just giving us a merry hand. See?"

"Well, I wish I could make something out of those signals. What do you suppose he means?"

"He doesn't mean anything. He's just playing."

"Well, why doesn't he just signal us to try the surf again—or go to sea and wait? If he told us to go south, or go to hell, there would be some reason in it. But look at him! He just stands there and spins his coat around like a wheel. That ass!"

"There come some more people."

"Oh, there's quite a mob there now. Look! Isn't that a boat?"

"Where? Oh, I see where you mean. No, that's no boat."

"That fellow is still waving his coat."

"He's an idiot. Why aren't they getting men to bring a boat out? A fishing boat—one of those big ones—could come out here all right. Why doesn't he do something?"

"Oh, it's all right now."

"They'll have a boat out here for us in less than no time—now that they've seen us."

A faint yellow tone came into the sky over the low land. The shadows on the sea slowly deepened. The wind became colder, and the men began to shiver.

"Holy smoke, what if we have to stay out here all night?" cried one of the men.

"Oh, we'll never have to stay here all night. They've seen us now. It won't be long before they'll come chasing out after us."

In the meantime, the oiler rowed and then the journalist rowed. And then the oiler rowed. The shape of the lighthouse had vanished from the southern horizon.

The sea to the east was black. The land had disappeared. The only sign of land now was the low and heavy thunder of the surf.

V

The cook was resting his head on the side of the boat. Without interest he watched the water just inches under his nose. Finally he spoke.

"Billie," he said dreamily, "what kind of pie do you like?"

"Pie!" said the oiler and the journalist angrily. "Don't talk about such things, blast you!"

"Well, I was just thinking about ham sandwiches and—" said the cook.

A night on the sea in an open boat is a long night. The plan that the oiler and the journalist had made was for one to row until he lost strength. Then he would wake the other one from his seawater couch in the bottom of the boat.

The oiler pulled the oars until his head drooped forward and sleep blinded him. Then he touched the man at the bottom of the boat and called his name softly. "Will you spell me for a little while?"

"Sure, Billie," the journalist said. He dragged himself to a sitting position. The two changed places carefully. Then the oiler sat down next to the cook. He seemed to go to sleep instantly.

The violence of the sea had stopped. Now the waves came without anger. The man at the oars had just one job. That was to keep the boat headed so that the tilt of the waves would not capsize her. The black waves were silent and hard to see in the darkness. A wave would almost be on top of the boat before the oarsman could even see it.

In a low voice, the journalist spoke to the captain. He was not sure that the captain was awake—although this iron man always seemed to be awake.

"Captain, shall I keep heading for that light to the north, sir?"

The same steady voice answered him. "Yes. Keep it about two points off the port bow."

As he rowed, the journalist looked down at the two men sleeping underfoot. The cook's arm was hanging over the oiler's shoulders. For a moment, the journalist was lost in his thoughts. Then suddenly there was a growling of water, and a wave roared into the boat. The cook continued to sleep. But the oiler sat up, blinking his eyes and shaking with the new cold.

"Oh, I'm very sorry, Billie," the journalist said.

"That's all right, old boy," the oiler said. He lay back down and in a moment was asleep again.

Before long it seemed that even the captain had dozed off. The journalist now felt that he was the one man afloat on all the ocean. The wind seemed to have a voice as it came over the waves. And it was sadder than the end.

Suddenly, there was a long, loud swishing sound behind the boat. A gleaming trail of light, like blue flame, could be seen on the black waters. It might have been made by a huge knife.

Then there was another swish and another long flash of bluish light. This time it was alongside the boat and might have been reached by an oar. The journalist saw a huge fin move like a shadow through the water. The giant fin hurled spray and left a long, glowing trail behind it.

The thing remained by the side of the boat. The speed and power of the thing was to be greatly admired. Somehow its presence did not affect the journalist with the sense of horror it might have. Still, it is true that he did not wish to be alone with it. He wished one of his companions was awake to keep him company. But the captain, the cook, and the oiler were all slumbering in the bottom of the boat.

VI

The thing that followed the boat had finally grown bored and gone away. One could no longer hear the slash of the cut water, nor see the flame of the long trail. The light in the north still glimmered, but it seemed no nearer to the boat.

Southward, someone had built a watch-fire on the beach. It was too low and too far away to be seen. But it made a shimmering reflection on the hills in back of it. That faint reflection could be seen from the boat.

The captain finally awoke and sat up. "Pretty long night," he said to the journalist. He looked at the shore. "Those life-saving people are taking their time."

"Did you see that shark playing around?" the journalist asked.

"Yes, I saw him," the captain answered. "He was a big fellow, all right."

"Wish I had known you were awake."

Later the journalist called softly into the bottom of the boat. "Billie." There was a slow and gradual stirring. "Billie, will you spell me?"

"Sure," said the oiler.

Later in the night they took the boat farther out to sea. The captain directed the cook to take one oar at the stern and keep the boat facing the sea. He told the cook to call out if he could hear the thunder of the surf. This plan allowed the oiler and the journalist to get some rest at the same time.

"We'll give those boys time to get in shape again," the captain said.

They curled down, and after a few trembles, slept the sleep of the dead. Neither knew they had left the cook in the company of another shark, or perhaps the same shark.

Soon, the cook spoke up. "Boys, she's drifted in pretty close. I guess one of you had better take her to sea again."

As the journalist took the oar once more, the captain gave him some whiskey and water. That helped to steady the chills out of him.

"If I ever get ashore and anybody even shows me a *picture* of an oar—"

At last there was a short conversation.

"Billie! Billie, will you spell me?"

"Sure," said the oiler.

VII

When the journalist opened his eyes again, the sea and sky were the gray color of dawn. Later, red and gold were painted upon the waters. Finally, the morning appeared in all its glory. The sky was pure blue and the sunlight flamed on the tips of the waves. On the distant shore, many little black cottages could be seen. A tall white windmill reared above them. No man, nor dog, nor bicycle appeared on the beach. The cottages might have formed a deserted village.

The voyagers scanned the shore. A meeting was held in the boat.

"Well, it looks like no help is coming. It might be better if we tried a run through the surf right away," the captain said. "If we stay out here much longer, we will be too weak to do anything for ourselves at all."

The others silently agreed.

"Now, boys, she is going to swamp for sure," the captain went on. "All we can do is work her in as far as possible. And then when she swamps, pile out and scramble for the beach. Keep cool now. Don't jump until she swamps for sure."

The oiler took the oars. Over his shoulder he scanned the surf. "Captain," he said, "I think I better bring her about. Then I'll try to keep her head-on to the seas and back her in."

"All right, Billie," the captain said. "Back her in."

The oiler swung the boat around. The huge waves heaved the boat high. Then once again the men were able to see the waters rushing upon the shore.

"We won't get in very close," said the captain.

Each time a man could turn his attention away from the waves, he glanced at the shore. The look on each man's face was covered in mystery. Looking at his mates, the journalist could tell they were not afraid. But he couldn't tell what they were thinking.

As for the journalist himself, he was too tired to think of much. He tried to force his mind into thinking of his survival. But the mind was being controlled by the muscles—and the muscles said that they did not care. The only thing that occurred to him was that if he should drown, it would be a shame.

"Now remember to get well clear of the boat when you jump," the captain said.

Then suddenly the crest of a wave fell with a thunderous crash. Another long sheet of white water came roaring down upon the boat.

"Steady now," the captain said.

The men were silent. They turned their eyes away from the shore and waited. The boat slid up a wave, leaped at the top, bounced over it, and then swung back down. The cook bailed out the water that had poured in.

The next wave crashed also. The tumbling, boiling flood of water caught the boat and whirled it around. Water swarmed in from all sides. The little boat, drunken with the weight of water, reeled and snuggled deeper into the sea.

"Bail her out, cook!" said the captain.

"All right, Captain," said the cook.

"Now boys, the next one will do us in for sure," said the oiler. "Get ready to jump clear of the boat."

The third wave moved forward, big and angry. It seemed about to swallow the boat. At almost the same moment, the men fell into the sea. A piece of life-belt had been lying in the bottom of the boat. As the journalist went overboard, he held this to his chest with his left hand.

The January water was icy. The journalist hadn't expected water off the coast of Florida to be so cold. To his dazed mind, that seemed an important fact to remember. The coldness of the water was sad, tragic. This fact was somehow mixed and confused with his feelings about his own situation. It almost seemed like a good reason for tears. The water was very cold.

When he came to the surface, the journalist was conscious of little but the noisy water. Then he saw his mates in the sea. The oiler was ahead in the race. He was swimming strongly and rapidly. Off to the journalist's left, the cook's great white back bulged out of the water. In the rear, the captain was hanging onto the keel of the overturned boat.

The journalist paddled slowly. At times he was able to ride down the crest of a wave. But then he arrived at a place where the travel was difficult. He did not stop swimming to find out what kind of current had caught him. But his progress stopped. The shore seemed to be set before him like scenery on a stage. He looked at it and understood every detail.

As the cook passed much farther to the left, the captain was calling to him. "Turn over on your back, cook! Turn over on your back and use the oar."

"All right, sir." The cook turned on his back. Then, paddling with an oar, he shot ahead as if he himself were a canoe.

Soon the boat also passed to the left of the journalist. The captain was still clinging with one hand to the keel. The little boat was being tossed and turned, pushed up and slammed down by the waves. The journalist marveled that the captain could still hold onto it.

The strange current still held the journalist in its grip. The shore was spread before him like a picture. It was coming very near to him. Yet still he thought, "Am I going to drown? Can it be possible? Can it be possible?" No doubt any man considers his own death the final act of nature.

A while later, another wave whirled him out of the small, deadly current. Suddenly the journalist found that he could make progress toward the shore. Later still he was aware that the captain had turned his face away from the shore and toward him. "Come to the boat, come to the boat," the captain was calling to him.

The journalist struggled to reach the captain and the boat. Presently, he saw a man running along the shore. The man was undressing with great speed. Coat, pants, shirt, everything flew magically off him.

"Come to the boat!" the captain called.

"All right, Captain."

As the journalist paddled, he saw the captain leave the boat. Right then the journalist performed his one little marvel of the voyage. A large wave caught him. It flung him with ease completely over the boat and far beyond it. It struck him as a true miracle of the sea.

The journalist arrived in water that reached only to his waist. But his condition did not permit him to stand for more than a minute. Each wave knocked him into a heap, and the undertow pulled at him.

Then he saw the man who had been undressing come running into the water. He dragged ashore the cook, and then waded toward the captain. But the captain waved him away and sent him toward the journalist. The man was naked—as naked as a tree in winter. But he had a halo about his head and he shone like a saint.

The man gave a strong pull and a long drag at the journalist's hand. The journalist could only say, "Thanks, old man."

But suddenly the naked man cried, "What's that?" He pointed his finger.

The journalist said, "Go."

In the shallow water, face downward, lay the oiler. His forehead touched sand that, between each rolling wave, was clear of the sea.

The journalist did not know all that happened afterward. When he reached safe ground, he fell. Then he, too, struck the sand with every part of his body. It was as if he had dropped from a roof.

Instantly it seemed that the beach was filled with men and women. They carried blankets, clothes, flasks, and coffee pots. The welcome of the land to the men from the sea was warm and generous. But then a still and dripping shape was carried slowly up the beach. The land's welcome for it was only the cold hospitality of the grave.

When the night came, the white waves paced to and fro in the moonlight. The wind brought the sound of the great sea's voice to the men on the shore. Now they felt that they could understand it and tell others what it was saying.

※

The Bride Comes to Yellow Sky

The showdown between the lawman and the gunslinger is one of the favorite legends of the Old West. In this story, there's an added twist. An out-of-control cowboy is spoiling for a fight. Until now, the town marshal has always met his challenge. Why should today be any different?

"HAVE YOU EVER BEEN IN A PARLOR CAR BEFORE?" HE
ASKED, SMILING WITH DELIGHT.

The Bride Comes to Yellow Sky

The great train moved west across the Texas plains. Long flats of green grass flew by. Woods of light and tender trees and little groups of frame houses all swept to the east.

A newly married couple had boarded the train in San Antonio. The man's red face showed that most of his life had been spent in the wind and sun. He was wearing the new black clothes he had bought for his wedding. From time to time, he looked down respectfully at his clothes. He sat with a hand on each knee, like a man waiting in a barber's shop. The look he gave other passengers was secretive and shy.

The bride was not pretty, nor was she very young. For the train trip she had chosen a blue cashmere dress. It had many touches of velvet and dozens of steel buttons. Every once in a while she would twist her head to look at her puff sleeves. They were very stiff, straight, and high. Somehow those sleeves embarrassed her. Her hands made it quite clear that she had worked hard. The look on her face made it equally clear that she expected to go on working hard as her duty.

The couple was obviously very happy. "Have you ever been in a parlor car before?" he asked, smiling with delight.

"No," she answered. "I never was. It's fine, isn't it?"

"Great! After a while we'll go forward to the diner and get a big layout. We'll get the finest meal in the world. They charge a dollar."

"Oh, do they?" cried the bride. "Charge a dollar? Why, that's too much for us—ain't it, Jack?"

"Not this trip, anyhow," he answered bravely. "We're going to go the whole thing."

Later, he explained to her about the trains. "You see, it's 1,000 miles from one end of Texas to the other. And this train runs right across. It only stops four times."

Then, as if he owned the train, he pointed out the dazzling features of the coach. Her eyes opened wider as she studied their surroundings. She saw sea-green figured velvet, shining brass and silver, and wood as shiny as a pool of oil.

To the minds of the pair, their grand surroundings reflected their feelings. They had just been married that morning in San Antonio. The man's face in particular fairly beamed with

happiness. That look made him appear
ridiculous to the black porter who
watched them from afar. He wore an
amused and superior grin. Many other
passengers in the car also watched the
couple with the same kind of smiles.

"We are due in Yellow Sky at 3:42," the
new husband said, looking tenderly into
his wife's eyes.

"Oh, are we?" she said, as if she had
not been aware of it. To show surprise at
her husband's statement was part of her
attempt to be a good wife. Then she took
a little silver watch from her pocket. As
she held it before her and studied its
face, her new husband's face shone.

"I bought it in San Anton' from a friend
of mine," he told her proudly.

"It's 17 minutes past 12," she said
shyly.

At last they went to the dining car. Two
rows of black waiters in shiny white suits
watched them enter with interest. The
pair went to the table of a waiter who

took pleasure in steering them through their meal. His face shone with fatherly kindness. They were not aware that he was having a bit of fun with them. Yet, as they returned to their coach, their faces showed a great sense of relief.

To the left of the train, down a long purple slope, a ribbon of mist hung over the Rio Grande. The train was coming toward the river at an angle. At the top of the next rise was the town of Yellow Sky. As the train got closer to the town, the husband grew more restless. His brick-red hands moved in a nervous way. Sometimes his mind wandered even when his bride leaned forward to talk to him.

To tell the truth, Jack Potter had a lot on his mind. He was beginning to feel the shadow of a deed weighing down on him. Potter was the town marshal of Yellow Sky. He was a man who was well known, liked, and feared in his corner—an important person. He had gone to San

Antonio to meet a girl he loved. And there, after the usual prayers, he had actually convinced her to marry him. But he had completed the entire act without letting anyone in Yellow Sky know about it. Now he was bringing his new bride home to an innocent and unsuspecting town.

Of course the other people of Yellow Sky married as it pleased them. But Potter thought that he had a higher duty to his friends. Now he was feeling that he had committed a great crime. He had been face to face with this girl in San Antonio. And he had gone headlong over all the social hedges! In San Antonio, he was like a man hidden in the dark. He could do whatever he pleased. But the hour of Yellow Sky—the hour of daylight—was coming fast.

Potter knew full well that his marriage would be an important thing to the town. His friends could not forgive him. Often he had thought about telling them by telegraph. But he had backed away from that idea again and again. And now the train was rushing him toward a scene of amazement, celebration, and dishonor.

Yellow Sky had a kind of brass band. The musicians played painfully, to the delight of the townspeople. Potter laughed without heart as he thought of it. If only the citizens of the town knew that he was arriving with his bride! They would surely parade the band at the train station. Then they would escort the new couple—amid cheers and congratulations—to their home.

He decided to make a quick trip from the station to his house. There they would be safe. Only then would he tell anyone about the wedding. Then he'd stay out of sight until his friends had time to lose a little of their enthusiasm.

The bride looked anxiously at him. "What's worrying you, Jack?"

He laughed again. "I'm not worrying, girl. I'm only thinking of Yellow Sky."

She flushed in an understanding way.

The sense of guilt that invaded both of their minds only increased their tenderness. They looked at each other with glowing eyes. But again, Potter laughed the same nervous laugh. And the flush upon the bride's face seemed quite permanent.

"We're nearly there," he said.

Then the porter came and announced the upcoming stop at Yellow Sky. The man slowly turned this way and that way as he brushed Potter's new clothes. Potter took out a coin and gave it to the porter. He had seen other passengers do this.

The porter took their bag. As the train began to slow, the couple moved forward to the hooded platform of the car. Soon the two engines pulled their long string of coaches into the Yellow Sky station.

"They have to take on water here," Potter said, as if that were an important piece of information. He had a very tight throat. Before the train stopped, he had quickly looked over the length of the platform. He was glad and astonished to see that there was no one on it but the station agent. When the train halted, the porter hopped off first. He placed a little temporary step on the ground.

"Come on, girl," Potter said to his wife. As he helped her down, they each laughed in a false way. Then he took the bag from the porter, and his wife clung to his arm. As they hurried away, he saw that their two trunks were being unloaded. Then he saw the station agent running toward him, making gestures. Potter laughed and groaned at the same time. So this was the first effect of his marriage upon Yellow Sky! He gripped his wife's arm firmly to his side, and they fled.

* * *

The California express on the Southern Railway was due at Yellow Sky in 21 minutes. Six men were at the bar of the Weary Gentleman saloon. One was a salesman. He talked fast and without stopping. Three of the men were Texans who did not care to talk at that time. And two were Mexican sheepherders, who made a general practice of not talking at all in the Weary Gentleman saloon.

The barkeeper's dog lay on the boardwalk in front of the door. His head was on his paws. He looked sleepily here and there with the constant care of a dog that is kicked sometimes. At the cooler end of the railway station, a man tilted back in a chair and smoked his pipe. Except for the busy salesman and his friends in the saloon, Yellow Sky seemed to be dozing.

The salesman was in the middle of telling a long-winded story. Then suddenly a young man rushed in the open door. "Scratchy Wilson's drunk," he said. "He's turned loose with both hands!" At that, the two Mexicans set down their glasses. They faded out the rear entrance of the saloon as if they were suddenly in a big hurry.

The salesman was innocent and in a good mood. "All right, old man—suppose he has?" he said. "Come in and have a drink, anyhow."

But the information seemed to have dented every skull in the room. Even the salesman was soon forced to see its importance. The mood in the room had become instantly serious.

"Say, what *is* this?" he asked.

The young man who brought the news turned to answer him. "It means, my friend, that for the next two hours, this town won't be a health resort."

The barkeeper rushed to the door. He locked and barred it. Then, reaching out the window, he pulled in heavy wooden shutters and barred them, too. That put a chapel-like gloom on the place. The salesman looked quickly from one man to another.

"Say, what *is* this, anyhow?" he cried. "You don't mean there is going to be a gunfight?"

"Don't know whether there'll be a fight or not," answered one man. "But there'll be some shootin'—some *good* shootin'."

The young man who had just come in waved his hand. "Oh, there'll be a fight fast enough—if anyone wants it. *Anybody* can get a fight out there in the street. There's a fight just waiting."

The salesman seemed to be torn. On the one hand, he had the sharp interest of an outsider. On the other, he had a feeling of personal danger.

"What did you say his name was?" he asked.

"Scratchy Wilson," the group of men announced together.

"And will he kill anybody? What are you going to do? Does this happen often? Does he carry on like this once a week or so? Can he break in that door?"

"No, he can't break down that door," replied the barkeeper. "He's tried it three times. But when he comes, you'd better lie down on the floor, stranger. He's dead sure to shoot at it—and a bullet *may* come through."

After that the salesman kept a close eye upon the door. It was not time yet for him to hug the floor. But just to be safe, he sidled over to the wall. "Will he kill anybody?" he asked in a small voice.

The other men laughed scornfully at the question.

"He's out to shoot, and he's out for trouble," one of them said. "Don't see any good taking any chances with him."

"But what do you do in a case like this? What do you *do*?" the salesman asked.

"Why, he and Jack Potter—" the bartender said.

"But Jack Potter's in San Anton'," the others reminded him.

"Well, who is Potter? And what's he got to do with it?" the salesman asked.

"Oh, he's the town marshal. He goes out and fights Scratchy when he goes on one of these sprees," one of the Texans explained.

"Wow!" said the salesman, mopping his brow. "Nice job he's got."

Then the voices died away to just whisperings. The salesman wished to ask more questions. But when he tried to, the men just frowned and motioned him to be quiet. A tense waiting hush was upon them.

In the deep shadows of the room, their eyes shone as they listened for sounds from the street. One man made three gestures at the barkeeper. Moving like a ghost, the man handed him a glass and a bottle. Then, without a sound, the barkeeper took a Winchester rifle from beneath the bar. A moment later, he motioned to the salesman to come over to him. The man tiptoed across the room.

"You better come with me back of the bar," the bartender whispered.

"No thanks," the salesman said, sweating. "I'd rather stay where I could make a break for the back door."

Then the man who had ordered the whiskey made another gesture. The salesman obeyed it—and found himself seated on a box behind the bar. In front of him were various metal fittings that looked a lot like protective armor plate. The barkeeper sat comfortably on a box next to him.

"You see, this here Scratchy Wilson is a wonder with a gun," the barkeeper whispered. "When he goes on the war path, we look for our holes—naturally. He's about the last one of the old gang that used to hang out along the river here. He's a terror when he's drunk.

When he's sober he's all right. In fact, he's the nicest fellow in town. Wouldn't hurt a fly! But when he's drunk—whoo!"

No one said anything for a while. Then the bartender spoke up again. "I wish Jack Potter was back from San Anton'. He had to shoot Wilson once—in the leg. Potter would know just what to do. He would sail in and pull out the kinks in this thing."

Then they heard a distant sound of a shot, followed by three wild yowls. The gunfire shattered the silence in the darkened saloon. There was a shuffling of feet. The men all looked at each other. "Here he comes," they said.

* * *

The wide-eyed man wore a maroon-colored shirt that he had bought purely for the decoration. He rounded a corner and walked into the middle of the main street of Yellow Sky. In each hand he held a long, heavy, blue-black revolver.

As he walked along, the man often yelled. These cries echoed through what seemed to be a deserted village. The surrounding stillness was like the arch of a tomb over him. His cries of wild challenge rang against these walls of silence.

Scratchy Wilson's face flamed in a rage caused by whiskey. His eyes were rolling and yet looking for ambush at the same time. They restlessly hunted the still doorways and windows. The man walked with the creeping movement of the midnight cat. He handled the long revolvers as if they were as light as straws. The cords of his neck stuck out and sank back, stuck out and sank back, as passion moved him.

There was no offer of a fight—no offer at all. Scratchy called to the sky. There were no takers. He bellowed and fumed and waved his revolvers here and there and everywhere.

The barkeeper's dog had not noticed the turn of events. He lay sleeping in front of his master's door. At the sight of the dog, the man paused and raised his revolver in a joking way. At the sight of the man, the dog jumped up. Then he walked slowly away, with a sad-faced growl.

The man yelled, and the dog broke into a gallop. Just as he was about to enter an alley, the dog heard a loud noise and a whistling. Then something spat on the ground right in front of his face. The dog howled, turned in terror, and galloped headlong in a new direction. Scratchy Wilson stood laughing, his weapons at his side.

Finally, the man was attracted by the closed door of the Weary Gentleman saloon. He went to it and, hammering with a revolver, demanded a drink.

The door remained shut. Scratchy picked up a bit of paper from the walk, and stuck it on the door frame with a knife. He then turned his back on the place and walked across the street. There, he spun on his heel quickly and fired at the piece of paper. He missed it by a half-inch. He swore at himself and wandered off. Later, he shot up the windows of several other places. The man was playing with the town. It was a toy for him.

Still, there was no offer of fight. Then the name of Jack Potter, his old enemy, entered his mind. Scratchy Wilson decided that it would be a good thing to go to Potter's house. If he made enough noise, maybe he could force Potter to come out and fight.

When the man got there, Potter's house presented a quiet, still front. It was the same as all the other houses in town. Scratchy took up a position and then howled a challenge. But the house, like a great stone god, just looked at him. It gave no sign. After a decent wait, the man howled further challenges. This time he mixed them with wonderful insults.

Soon, the drunken man was churning himself into deep rage. He fumed at the stillness of the house as the winter wind attacks a prairie cabin in the North. His shouts and curses were a terrible thing to hear. In the distance, it might have sounded like the fighting of 200 cowboys. As necessary, Scratchy Wilson paused for breath or to reload his revolvers.

* * *

Potter and his bride walked somewhat shyly but with great speed. "Next corner, dear," he said finally.

The bridegroom was about to raise a finger to point out their new home. Then, as the pair circled the corner, they came face to face with a wild-looking man in a maroon-colored shirt. He was feverishly pushing bullets into a large revolver. Quickly, the man dropped his revolver to the ground. Then, like lightning, he whipped another one from its holster. The second revolver was aimed at the bridegroom's chest.

There was a silence. Potter's mouth seemed to be no more than a grave for his tongue. He loosened his arm from the woman's grip. The bag he was carrying dropped to the ground. As for the bride, her face had gone as yellow as old cloth.

The two men faced each other at a distance of three paces. The man with the revolver smiled with quiet force.

"Tried to sneak up on me," he said. "Tried to sneak up on me!" The look in his eyes grew more evil. As Potter made a slight movement, the man thrust his revolver forward. "No, don't you do it, Jack Potter. Don't you move a finger toward a gun just yet. Don't you move an eyelash. The time has come for me to settle with you. And I'm going to do it my own way. So, if you don't want a gun bent on you, just mind what I tell you."

Potter looked at his enemy. "I ain't got a gun on me, Scratchy," he said. "Honest, I ain't." He was stiffening and steadying. Yet somewhere in the back of his mind a picture of the train coach floated. He saw the velvet, the shining brass, the silver— the reflected glory of the marriage.

"You know I fight when it comes to fighting, Scratchy Wilson. But I ain't got a gun on me. You'll have to do all the shootin' yourself."

His enemy's face went darker red with rage. He stepped forward. Then he lashed his weapon back and forth in front of Potter's chest.

"Don't tell me you ain't got no gun on you," Scratchy Wilson said. "Don't tell me no lie like that. There ain't a man in Texas ever seen you without a gun. Don't take me for no kid."

"I ain't taking you for no kid," Potter answered. His heels had not moved an inch backward. "I'm taking you for a

damn fool. I tell you I ain't got a gun—
and I ain't. If you're going to shoot me
up, you better do it now. You'll never get
a chance like this again."

The forced reasoning had taken a toll
on Wilson's rage. He was calmer. "If you
ain't got a gun—why ain't you got a gun?"
he sneered. "Been to Sunday school?"

"I ain't got a gun because I just came
from San Anton' with my wife. I'm
married," said Potter. "I had no idea there
was going to be any galoots like you
prowling around. If I had known you'd
be here when I brought my wife home,
I'd had a gun. And don't you forget it."

"Married!" said Scratchy, not at all
understanding.

"Yes, *married*. I'm married," Potter
said clearly.

"Married?" said Scratchy. Now, for the
first time, he seemed to see the drooping
woman at the other man's side. "No!"
he said. He was like a creature allowed

a peek into another world. He moved a pace backward. His arm, with the revolver, dropped to his side. "Is this the lady?" he asked.

"Yes, this is the lady," Potter answered.

There was another moment of silence.

"Well," said Wilson at last. "I suppose it's all off now."

"It's all off if you say so, Scratchy. You know I didn't make the trouble." Potter lifted his bag.

"Well, I'll allow it's off, Jack," Wilson said. He was looking at the ground. "Married!"

He had not decided to call off the fight because of respect for the marriage. It was just that—in the presence of this foreign condition—he was a simple child of the earlier plains. Scratchy Wilson picked up his revolver. Then, placing both weapons in their holsters, he went away. His feet made funnel-shaped tracks in the heavy sand.

Thinking About
the Stories

The Open Boat

1. How important is the background of the story? Is weather a factor in the story? Is there a war going on or some other unusual circumstance? What influence does the background have on the characters' lives?

2. Are there friends or enemies in this story? Who are they? What forces do you think keep the friends together and the enemies apart?

3. An author builds the plot around the conflict in a story. In this story, what forces or characters are struggling against each other? How is the conflict finally resolved?

The Bride Comes to Yellow Sky

1. Which character in this story do you most admire? Why? Which character do you like the least?

2. In what town, city, or country does this story take place? Is the location important to the story? Why or why not?

3. Look back at the illustration that introduces this story. What character or characters are pictured? What is happening in the scene? What clues does the picture give you about the time and place of the story?

8

LAKE CLASSICS

Great American Short Stories I

Washington Irving, Nathaniel Hawthorne, Mark Twain, Bret Harte, Edgar Allan Poe, Kate Chopin, Willa Cather, Sarah Orne Jewett, Sherwood Anderson, Charles W. Chesnutt

Great American Short Stories II

Herman Melville, Stephen Crane, Ambrose Bierce, Jack London, Edith Wharton, Charlotte Perkins Gilman, Frank R. Stockton, Hamlin Garland, O. Henry, Richard Harding Davis

Great British and Irish Short Stories

Arthur Conan Doyle, Saki (H. H. Munro), Rudyard Kipling, Katherine Mansfield, Thomas Hardy, E. M. Forster, Robert Louis Stevenson, H. G. Wells, John Galsworthy, James Joyce

Great Short Stories from Around the World

Guy de Maupassant, Anton Chekhov, Leo Tolstoy, Selma Lagerlöf, Alphonse Daudet, Mori Ogwai, Leopoldo Alas, Rabindranath Tagore, Fyodor Dostoevsky, Honoré de Balzac

Cover and Text Designer: Diann Abbott

Library of Congress Catalog Number: 94-075023
ISBN 1-56103-015-5
Printed in the United States of America
1 9 8 7 6 5 4 3 2 1

E CLASSICS

Great American
Short Stories II

❧

Stephen
CRANE

Stories retold by Tony Napoli
Illustrated by James Balkovek

LAKE EDUCATION
Belmont, California